Ronald Reagan

A Little Golden Book® Biography

By Lisa Rogers

Illustrated by Catherine Pape

🌷 A GOLDEN BOOK • NEW YORK

Text copyright © 2023 by Lisa Rogers
Cover art and interior illustrations copyright © 2023 by Catherine Pape
All rights reserved. Published in the United States by Golden Books, an imprint of Random
House Children's Books, a division of Penguin Random House LLC, 1745 Broadway, New York,
NY 10019. Golden Books, A Golden Book, A Little Golden Book, the G colophon, and
the distinctive gold spine are registered trademarks of Penguin Random House LLC.
rhcbooks.com
Educators and librarians, for a variety of teaching tools, visit us at RHTeachersLibrarians.com
Library of Congress Control Number: 2022942331
ISBN 978-0-593-64518-5 (trade) — ISBN 978-0-593-64519-2 (ebook)
Printed in the United States of America
10 9 8 7 6 5 4 3 2 1

Ronald Wilson Reagan was the 40th president of the United States of America.

Ronald was born on February 6, 1911, in the small town of Tampico, Illinois. His father worked hard as a shoe salesman. His mother helped others through her church.

Ronald and his family moved around a lot. They finally settled in Dixon, Illinois, when he was nine years old.

Ronald and his older brother, Neil, fished, swam, and played football. Their family didn't have a lot of money, but Ronald believed his future would be bright.

Ronald's mother taught him to read before he began school. He had a good memory and could easily remember things he read in books. He was a bright student and even skipped the second grade!

In high school, Ronald was captain of the football team. He also played basketball, ran track, and acted in school plays.

Ronald's friendliness and sense of humor made him popular with other students. They elected him class president.

After high school, Ronald went to Eureka College in Illinois. He still played football and acted in plays. Ronald won an acting award in a national competition. He knew then that he wanted to be an actor.

To help pay for college, Ronald worked during the summers as a lifeguard. He saved seventy-seven swimmers on the swift-moving Rock River!

The riverfront park is also where Ronald saddled up a horse for the first time. That big gray horse sparked a lifelong love of riding.

After college, Ronald got a job as a sports announcer for an Iowa radio station. He described the games so well that listeners felt like they were sitting on the bleachers.

The radio station sent him to California to report on the Chicago Cubs' spring training camp. While there, Ronald went to the Warner Bros. film studio and had an audition called a screen test. He did great!

Ronald's dream of becoming an actor was coming true. Right away, he got his first movie role—playing a radio announcer!

Throughout Ronald's acting career, he appeared in more than fifty films. He played a professor, a news reporter, a cowboy, even a submarine commander. His favorite roles were ones in which he rode horses!

In one film, Ronald played a football star named George Gipp. George couldn't compete because of an illness and asked his teammates to "win just one for the Gipper." The Gipper became Ronald's nickname.

SCENE 3   TAKE 1   ROLL 2

PROD | KNUTE ROCKNE ALL AMERICAN
DIRECTOR | LLOYD BACON
CAMERA | A

Ronald met his first wife, Jane Wyman, while filming a movie together. The couple married in 1940 and raised two children, Maureen and Michael. They ended their marriage in 1949.

A few years later, Ronald married Nancy Davis. She was also an actor. They had a daughter, Patti, and a son, Ronald Prescott. Nancy was the love of Ronald's life and his best friend.

Ronald joined the Screen Actors Guild, a union which sought good working conditions for actors. Soon he was elected its president.

Ronald led the union on a strike. He and the other actors refused to work until the movie studios agreed to make changes. Ronald was proud of his leadership. Some of those changes still benefit actors today.

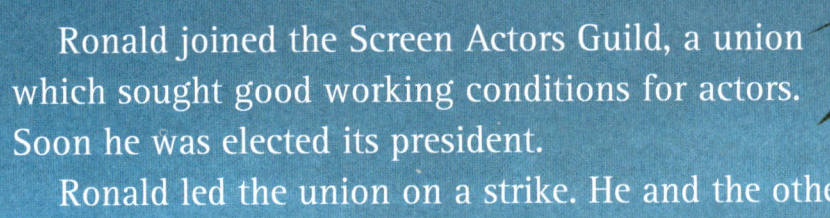

In 1954, Ronald got a job as host of the *General Electric Theater* television show. The company General Electric also asked him to give speeches to its workers.

Ronald listened to the workers' ideas about how to improve their lives. They thought they should be able to keep more of the money they earned rather than pay high taxes. They wanted more of a say in government, too. Ronald agreed.

   As Ronald gave speeches throughout the country,
he became more interested in politics than acting. He
decided to run for governor of California.

   Ronald won the election and served as governor
from 1967 to 1975. That's also when he started eating
lots and lots of jelly beans. His favorite flavor? Licorice!

In 1979, Ronald entered the race for president. He thought the country needed his leadership. He ran against the current president, Jimmy Carter.

Ronald pledged to help people get jobs and make the United States safer and more respected around the world. He asked voters to "help win one for the Gipper."

People liked his ideas for a stronger, better America. They also liked the folksy, direct way he talked to them. He gained another nickname, the Great Communicator.

Ronald won the election and was sworn in as president of the United States on January 20, 1981, with Nancy by his side.

President Ronald Reagan created jobs and invested in space technology, including plans to build the International Space Station. He appointed the first woman, Sandra Day O'Connor, to the United States Supreme Court.

He also enjoyed celebrating Americans' accomplishments. He gave a speech at the opening of the 1984 Olympics in Los Angeles, asking athletes to do their best—for themselves and their country.

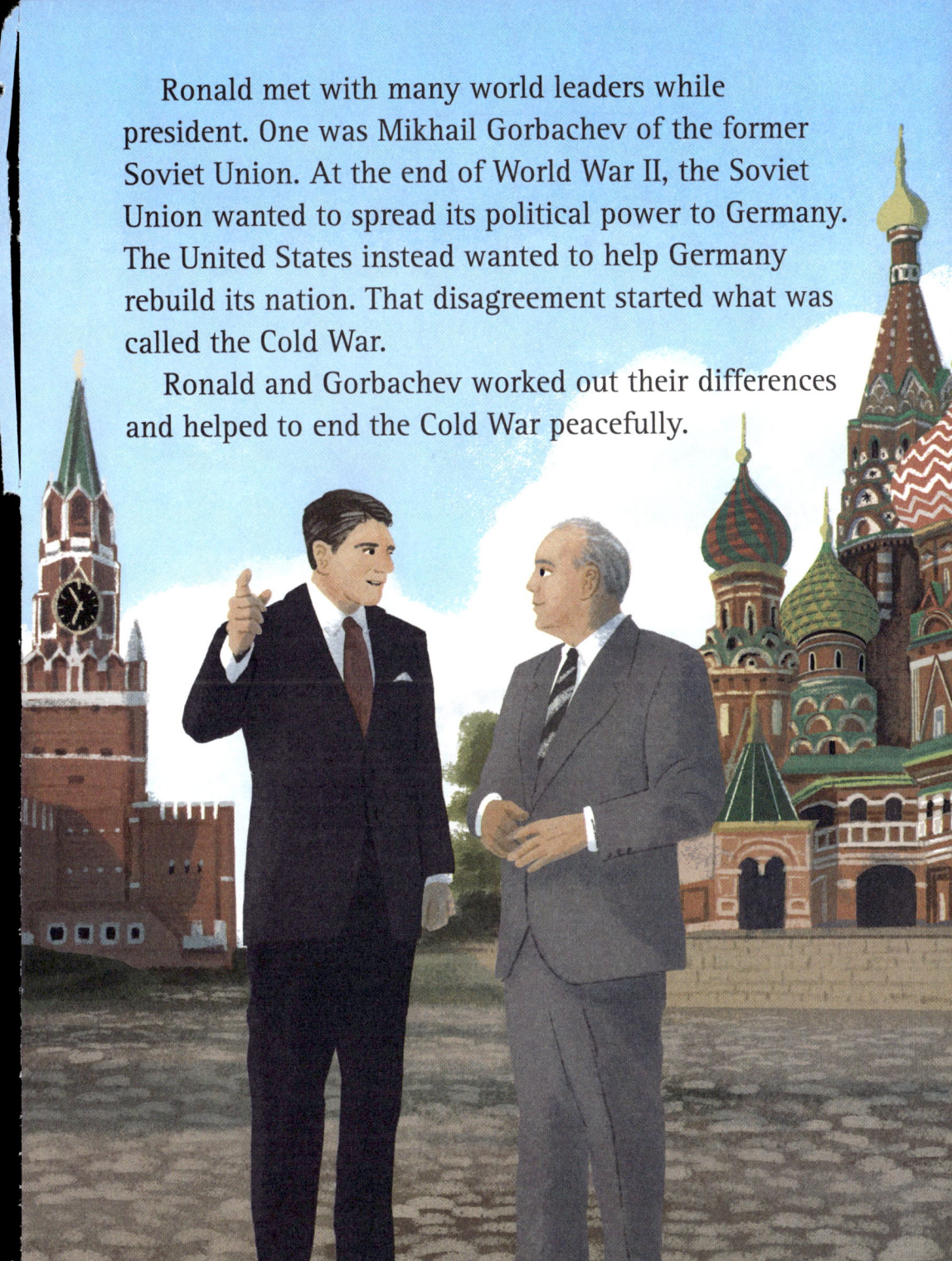

Ronald met with many world leaders while president. One was Mikhail Gorbachev of the former Soviet Union. At the end of World War II, the Soviet Union wanted to spread its political power to Germany. The United States instead wanted to help Germany rebuild its nation. That disagreement started what was called the Cold War.

Ronald and Gorbachev worked out their differences and helped to end the Cold War peacefully.

In 1984, Ronald was reelected for a second term. On January 20, 1989, Ronald's presidency came to an end. Ronald went home to his California ranch, where he and Nancy rode horses. During retirement, he gave speeches and wrote a book about his life. He received awards, including the Presidential Medal of Freedom, which was given to him by President George H. W. Bush.

In 1994, Ronald wrote a letter to the American
people telling them he had Alzheimer's, a disease that
affects the brain and makes it hard to remember things.
He hoped that by sharing this, he might help others
affected by the disease.

Ronald Reagan died on June 5, 2004. His belief in hard work and his ability to connect with people helped him rise from his humble beginnings to become president of the United States.

Ronald was proud of his accomplishments and honored to have been president of our great country. He always believed America's future was bright.

"LIVE EACH DAY WITH ENTHUSIASM, OPTIMISM, HOPE, AND HONOR."